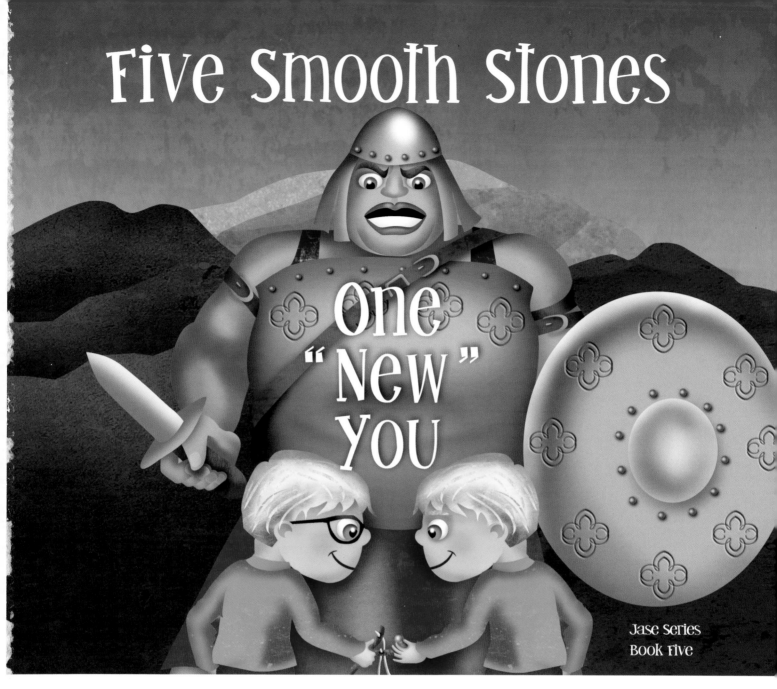

Five Smooth Stones

One "New" You

Jase Series
Book Five

Written by Jason Crabb
Illustrated by Anita DuFalla

Printed in the United States of America   ISBN 978-0-9888994-4-5   www.jasoncrabb.com

The JASE Series is dedicated to my girls: my beautiful wife, Shellye,
and our precious daughters, Ashleigh and Emma. You mean the world to me.
With love from our family to yours:
Jason, Ashleigh, Shellye, and Emma.

Special thanks to Philip and Tina Morris and Donna Scuderi for your creative input and love of the cause.

Number
5

The 5th Commandment

All children and crabs, respect Mom and Dad.

1. Love God more than all, even crabs great and small.

2. Friend and crab, while you love them, always see God above them.

3. Don't be crabby toward God. Say His name with your love.

4. God's day of rest is for you — and for your crab, too.

5. All children and crabs, respect Mom and Dad.

6. Don't hurt one another, not a crab or your brother.

7. Crab or person alike: love your husband or wife.

8. Never steal from your brother, your crab, or another.

9. Little boys, girls, and crabs, tell the truth and be glad.

10. Be sure to enjoy your stuff and your crab, not wishing for something your neighbor has.

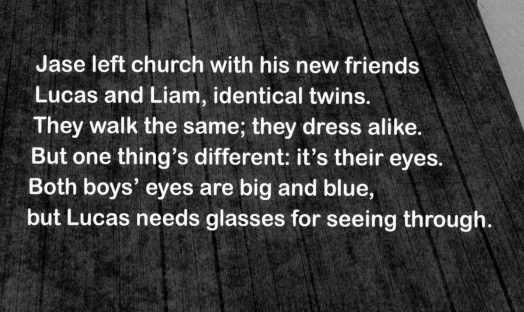

Jase left church with his new friends
Lucas and Liam, identical twins.
They walk the same; they dress alike.
But one thing's different: it's their eyes.
Both boys' eyes are big and blue,
but Lucas needs glasses for seeing through.

Jase asked, "Lucas, do you think that you could teach me to use a slingshot, too?"

"Sure," he answered, "I'll show you how, but maybe later, not right now."

Behind Lucas' glasses, his eyes looked small like distant, blue, bouncing balls.

Lucas seemed preoccupied,
and soon lagged far behind.

His dad said, "Come on, son. Stay close."

But Lucas never seemed to notice.

6

Jase asked Liam, "Is Lucas sad?"

Liam answered, "Well…sometimes…yes.
Lucas is so smart and kind,
but he worries about his eyes.
He feels hurt by other kids
who think that he is 'different.'"

Suddenly, Jase knew
exactly what he was sent to do.
God wanted him to help young Lucas
see himself with a fresh new focus.

When they got home, Jase asked if they could go out in the yard and play.

The twins' mom said, "Why, yes, of course! Please make yourself at home with us!"

"Then let's shoot pebbles at a can," said Jase to Lucas and Liam.

Liam agreed. "Yes, please, Lucas!
There's so much that you can teach us.
I can shoot stones, but not like you—"

"And," Jase added, "I haven't a clue!"
Lucas said, "Okay, I guess.
I'll help. At least I'll try my best."

Lucas explained what to do.
Then he showed them how
to shoot.
Stone by stone, Lucas aimed.

"All perfect shots!" Jase
exclaimed.

Lucas said, "I did okay,
but I can't play in other games.
The kids I know think I can't see,
so they choose Liam over me."

"That doesn't make
them right, you know.
They cannot limit where
you go.
Whatever God has
planned for you
is way too big for them
or you!"

"Do you know David, the shepherd lad?"
"No," they answered, "Who is that?"

"That young man changed history
by killing a giant. Let's go see!"

14

"His brothers thought him much too young
to be important to anyone.
They left him alone with his 'few sheep'
while they went off to war with the king."
(1 Samuel 17:28)

15

"But Goliath, their enemy, made them afraid.
They trembled when they heard his name.
He was at least nine feet tall,
and in their minds, they felt small."

16

"But when David stopped by to bring supplies,
he looked Goliath in the eye.
He vowed he'd defeat the giant that day
no matter who laughed or said, "No way!"
With five smooth stones and a sling
to shoot,

David ran at the giant

as though *David* were huge."

"David shot just one
smooth stone
and instantly, Goliath
moaned.

The evil giant had been
defeated,
by a boy they said could
never beat him."

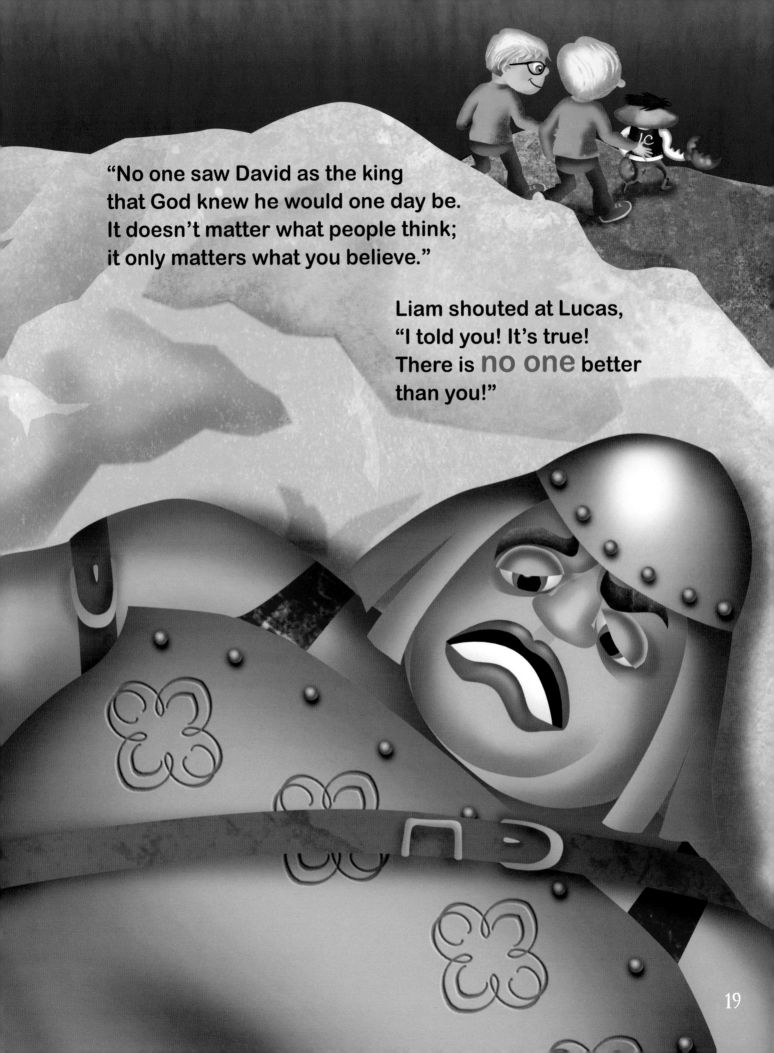

"No one saw David as the king
that God knew he would one day be.
It doesn't matter what people think;
it only matters what you believe."

Liam shouted at Lucas,
"I told you! It's true!
There is no one better
than you!"

19

"Now I get it!" Lucas said.
"But it's getting late and out of respect
we had better hurry home.
We have to clean our room."

"Hey," Jase said, "that's the fifth commandment to
always **love** and **respect** your parents!"

Back at home the cleaning started. Mom
and dad helped with the task.
The twins' dad thought of something.

He said, "I watched you in the yard,"
taking turns with the slingshot.
It looked like fun, so let's invite
other kids to take a try."

"Really, Dad? Invite the kids
who never let me play with them?
You think they'll come? And will they play
a baseball game with me one day?"

"Sure!" said Jase. "Let's have a party."

Dad replied, "Your birthday's coming!

We'll have some **cake** and **songs** to **sing**.

Your friends will learn to use your sling."

Several days later…
"Okay, kids, let's play a game
of shooting stones and taking aim.
Finish your cake. Start lining up
to shoot the can there on the stump."

So everyone got
in line
to take three sling shots
at a time.

Jase made sure
the can was set
each time
someone shot at it.
Liam went first and
hit it twice.
Lucas hit it all
three times!

"Wow!" said the kids, "Can
you teach us that, too?
And Lucas said, "Sure, I'll do
that for you!"

25

"Just stand very still, and draw the sling back.
It is just as easy as that!
Let go of the sling and the stone will sail
straight into the can or even a pail."

One of the boys who liked to play ball
had watched in amazement and thought about all
the ways that Lucas could help his team.
He asked, "Will you play ball with the guys and me?"

"Sure," said Lucas, "I'd love to play.
Thanks for asking! When's the next game?"

"It's Tuesday night. Bring a mitt.
I'll bet you can pitch with the best of them.

Lucas was thrilled to finally be
invited to play on somebody's team.
But just when fresh joy flooded his heart,
he saw a boy standing alone and apart.

"What's wrong?" Lucas asked. "Are you okay?"

"I'm a little shy; I'm from far away.
Your mother was kind to invite me to come.
But my accent is strong. I don't know anyone."

"Ah," said Jase. "I understand.
I'm not like Anyone in this land!"

"Hey," said Lucas, "Jase could be a friend to you like he's been to me."

"Now there's an idea," said Jase. "I predict..."

"…amazing things ahead in Book Six!"

Jase® — A "Crabb" With a Mission

Children are precious — to us and to God! And their growing-up years are so important to the people they become. Through their everyday experiences, children discover their individual identities, their unique destinies, and the reality of their loving Creator.

When faced with challenges and disappointments, children are comforted to learn that other children share many of the same experiences. As they hear other children's stories, they are strengthened in discovering that they are not alone, or "more strange," or "less courageous" than their peers.

The vision for The Jase® Series took root in my heart two decades ago. Now, as a husband and the father of two beautiful girls, I long to reach children and those who love and care for them with the Good News—the gospel of Jesus Christ! I pray that this children's story will sing the melody of God's heart to yours, whatever your age.

— Jason Crabb

coming up next in the Jase series

In a continuing dreamland adventure, Jase® and his friend Ranjeet see Jesus' Sermon on the Mount, and learn what it means to have a pure heart.

Hey kids!

Now that you've read the book, how would you like to:

- Download Jase FUN pages
- Access the Jase and You Review
- Earn a diploma from Jase University
- And more ...

Go with me to www.jasecrabb.com to continue our journey together!!!